The Boublil–Schönberg Collection

Show Hits

Twelve great show songs ideal for auditions

C014542988

This publication is not authorised for sale in the
United States of America and/or Canada.

Wise Publications
part of The Music Sales Group
London/New York/Paris/Sydney/Copenhagen/Berlin/Madrid/Tokyo

Published by
Wise Publications
14/15 Berners Street, London W1T 3LJ, UK.

Exclusive Distributors:
Music Sales Limited
Distribution Centre, Newmarket Road, Bury St Edmunds, Suffolk IP33 3YB, UK.
Music Sales Corporation
257 Park Avenue South, New York, NY10010, USA.
Music Sales Pty Limited
20 Resolution Drive, Caringbah, NSW 2229, Australia.

Order No. AM983708
ISBN 1-84609-229-9

This book © Copyright 2005 Wise Publications,
a division of Music Sales Limited.

Cover design by Chloë Alexander
Printed in the United Kingdom

Your Guarantee of Quality
As publishers, we strive to produce every book to the highest commercial
standards.
This book has been carefully designed to minimise awkward page turns
and to make playing from it a real pleasure.
Particular care has been given to specifying acid-free, neutral-sized paper made
from pulps which have not been elemental chlorine bleached. This pulp is from
farmed sustainable forests and was produced with special regard for the
environment.
Throughout, the printing and binding have been planned to ensure a sturdy,
attractive publication which should give years of enjoyment.
If your copy fails to meet our high standards, please inform us and we will
gladly replace it.

www.musicsales.com

Also available:
The Boublil–Schönberg Collection
Show Hits
Audition Songs Female Edition
Twelve more show songs specially arranged for female singers complete with
backing tracks on CD.

Includes...
Castle On A Cloud Les Misérables
How Many Tears? Martin Guerre
I Dreamed A Dream Les Misérables
I Saw Him Once Les Misérables
I'd Give My Life For You Miss Saigon
The Movie In My Mind Miss Saigon
Now That I've Seen Her Miss Saigon
On My Own Les Misérables
Quatre Saisons Pour Un Amour La Révolution Française
The Sacred Bird Miss Saigon
Someone Martin Guerre
When Will Someone Hear? Martin Guerre

Order No. AM983719

The American Dream

Music and lyrics by
Claude-Michel Schönberg, Alain Boublil
& Richard Maltby Jr.

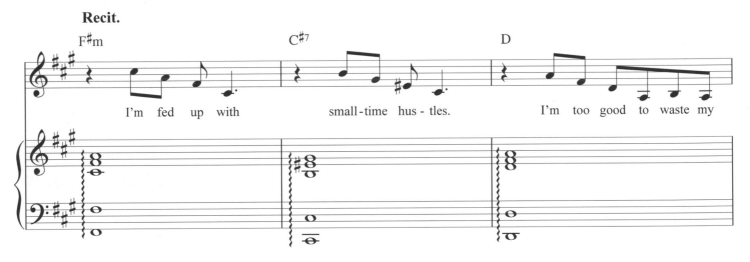

I'm fed up with small-time hus-tles. I'm too good to waste my

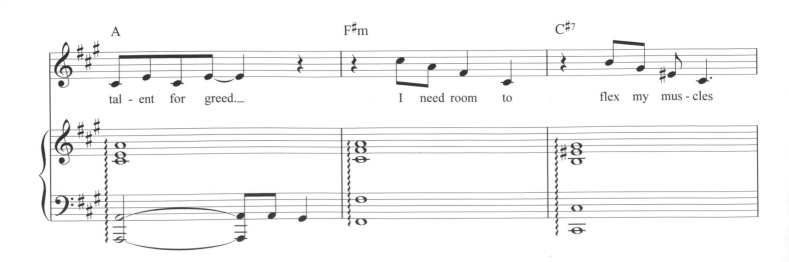

tal-ent for greed.___ I need room to flex my mus-cles

they have a law-yer and a bo-dy-guard.___ To the Johns there

I'll sell blondes there, that they can charge on a card.

Call girls are lin-ing Times Square, the A-me-ri-can dream.___

Bring Him Home

Music and lyrics by
Claude-Michel Schönberg, Alain Boublil & Herbert Kretzmer

CODA

Verse 2
Bring him peace, bring him joy.
He is young, he is only a boy.
You can take it. You can give.
Let him be. Let him live.
If I die, let me die.
Let him live. Bring him home,
Bring him home. Bring him home.

Bui-Doi

Music and lyrics by
Claude-Michel Schönberg, Alain Boublil & Richard Maltby Jr.

War is-n't ov - er when it ends, some pic - tures nev - er leave your
I nev - er thought one day I'd plead for half - breeds from a land that's

mind. They are the fa - ces___ of the child - ren, the ones we left be -
torn. But then I saw a camp for chil - dren whose crime was be - ing

- hind. }
born. } They're called Bui - Doi, the dust of

cresc.

mf

life. Con - ceived in hell and born in strife. { They are the
{ We owe them

living re - mind - ers of all the good we failed to do. That's why we
fa - thers and a fam - ily, a lov - ing home they nev - er knew. Be - cause we

know, deep in out hearts,___ that they're all our child - ren too.

These are souls in need, they need us to give.

Some - one has to pay for their chance to live. They're called Bui-

Empty Chairs At Empty Tables

Music and lyrics by
Claude-Michel Schönberg, Alain Boublil
& Herbert Kretzmer

Andante (♩ = 88)

There's a grief that can't be

spo - ken ___ There's a pain goes on and on ___

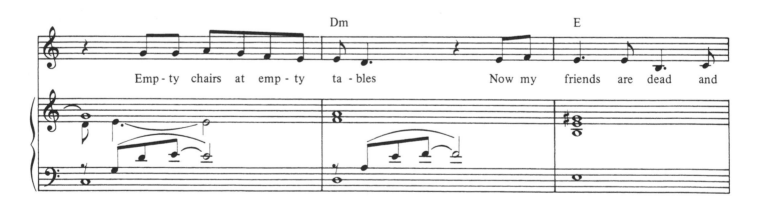

Emp - ty chairs at emp - ty ta - bles Now my friends are dead and

gone. Here they talked of re - vo - lu - tion ___

Do You Hear The People Sing?

Music and lyrics by
Claude-Michel Schönberg, Alain Boublil,
Jean-Marc Natel & Herbert Kretzmer

music of a peo - ple Who will not be slaves a - gain! When the

bea-ting of your heart Echoes the bea-ting of the drums, There is a life a-bout to start When to-mor-row

comes! Will you comes.

Here Comes The Morning

Music and lyrics by
Claude-Michel Schönberg, Alain Boublil
& Stephen Clark

free,   and   when   you have gone,   all I'll see   still   more

Più mosso - accel.

cold   nights—— of   wait - ing.   Days   all   a -

lone.   Kill- ing and   hat - ing,   but

A tempo

still —— there's   time —— for   you —— to learn, where -e -verthere are   dreams —— the fire —— of

mor - ning. And when the day is done, the

sun paints its last sil-hou - ettes. With luck, by the time that it

sets you'll be home.

Take your chance with o-pen eyes.

Is this my mor - ning? And when the
A man should love be - fore he dies.

day is done, the sun paints its last sil - hou - ettes. With
Ev'ry day the sun will rise.

luck, by the time that it sets you'll be home.

I Will Make You Proud

Music and lyrics by
Claude-Michel Schönberg, Alain Boublil,
Edward Hardy & Herbert Kretzmer

cursed but ne - ver cowed, in the call of du - ty, I will make you proud. Gas-

ton, I knew your fa - ther. Ma - ras, I knew yours too. Men who stoop for de - cen - cy

just the same as you. Sons, do not be - tray them, daugh - ters, do not fail.

In the face of pe — ril good - ness shall pre - vail. Stand up and be coun - ted,

we will root out this e - vil_____ in the name of the Lord. Ev - 'ry - where is cha - os, ev - 'ry - where is doubt, ev - 'ry - where are he - re - tics. The time has come to burn them out._____ In your hour of vict - 'ry

vow as I have vowed. Shout it from the roof - tops,

I will make you proud. Here I stand be - fore you,

blood - y and un - bowed. By the sword of Je - sus, I will make you

proud.

Martin Guerre

Music and lyrics by
Claude-Michel Schönberg, Alain Boublil
& Stephen Clark

E-nough, no more, I don't give a damn. Why stay? What for? I know who I am. A man a-bove the lie that we

live. A man who'll love when he's read-y to give. But I'll come back one day af-ter ten years a-

way and they'll stop and they'll say look!

Poco piu mosso

(Spoken) *Look*

Look,_____ it's__ Mar-tin

Guerre ____ we need him here. No need to fear, nev-er des-pair.

Yes ____ it's_ Mar-tin Guerre, ____ back home at last. Those from the past bet-ter be-

ware. Strides ____ through the town.

mf

Laughs! Waves them_a-way. They all ____ think he must be the

f

same, but by hea-ven they're sure to_ see there's more to___Mar-tin Guerre than a

Molto meno mosso (Colla voce)

name. And that bas-tard Pi-erre,

holds my life in his hands. He's no un-cle of mine. He can have all my land. The

Molto rit.

land he sold me for. May God con-demn his soul to hell and all of Ar-ti-gat as well.

Master Of The House

Music and lyrics by
Claude-Michel Schönberg, Alain Boublil,
Jean-Marc Natel & Herbert Kretzmer

Glad to do my friends a fa - vour ____ Does-n't cost me to be nice ____ but
Re - si -dents are more than wel - come ____ Bri - dal suite is oc - cu -pied! ____

no -thing gets you no -thing Ev - 'ry-thing has got a lit - tle price! ____
Rea -son -a -ble charg - es Plus ____ some lit -tle ex -tra on the side! ____

Mas - ter of the House   Keep-er of the zoo   Rea -dy to re -lieve them of a
Charge 'em for the lice   Ex -tra for the mice   Two per-cent for look-ing in the

sou, or two.   Wa -ter-ing the wine   Ma-king up the weight   Pick-ing up their knick-knacks When they
mir - ror twice!   Here a lit - tle slice   There a lit - tle cut   Three percent for sleep -ing with the

Ser - vant to the poor   But - ler to the great   Com - for - ter, phil - os - o - pher And

B7   E
life - long mate!   Eve - ry - bo - dy's boon com - pan - ion _____

C#   F#m   F#m/E   D   E7
Eve - ry - bo - dy's cha - pe - rone. ___   But   lock up your va - li - ses   Je -
Gives 'em eve - ry - thing he's got. ___   Dir - ty bunch of gee - zers   Je -

1.
A
- sus! Won't I skin yer to the bone!
- sus! What a sor - ry lit - tle

2.
A
lot!

Stars

Music and lyrics by
Claude-Michel Schönberg, Alain Boublil
& Herbert Kretzmer

door-way__ to Par-a-dise,__ That those who fal-ter, And those who fall Must

pay ____ the price . . .

Lord, let me find him, ___ That I may see him _____ Safe be-hind

bars. _____ I will ne-ver rest ___ Till then _____ This I

swear, This I swear by the stars. _____

49

Who Am I?

Music and lyrics by
Claude-Michel Schönberg, Alain Boublil,
Jean-Marc Natel & Herbert Kretzmer

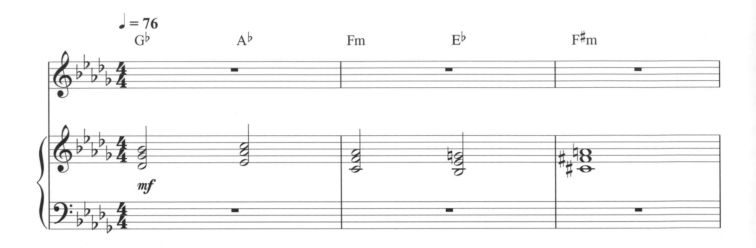

He thinks that man is me, he knew him at a

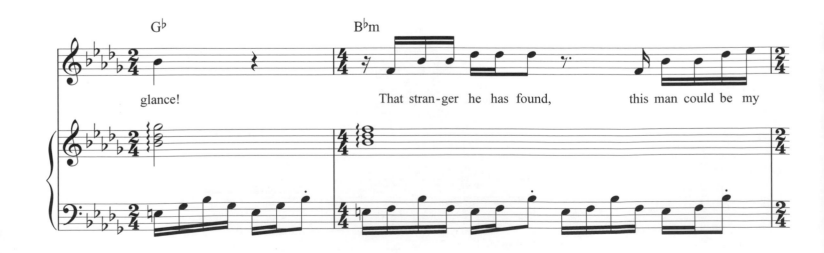

glance! That stran-ger he has found, this man could be my

chance.

Why should I save his hide, why should I right this

wrong?

When I have come so far and strug-gled for so

long.

If I speak I am con-demned.

If I stay si-lent I am damned.

Can I con-demn this man to sla-ve-ry, pre-tend I do not feel his a-go-ny? This in-no-cent who wears my face, who goes to judge-ment in my place, who am I?

Can I con-ceal my-self for-ev-er more, pre-tend I'm not the man I was be-fore? And must my name un-til I die be no more than an a-li-bi?

Must I lie?__ How can I ev-er face my fel-low man,__ how can I ev-er face my-self a-gain?

My soul be-longs to God, I know I made that bar-gain long a-go. He gave me hope when hope was gone. He gave me strength to jour-ney on. Who am I?

Who am I?

Why God Why?

Music and lyrics by
Claude-Michel Schönberg, Alain Boublil
& Richard Maltby Jr.

I can't help her,— no - one can. I liked my mem-'ries as they were but

now I'll leave— re - mem - b'ring her._____

When I went home be-fore,— no-one talked of the war.—

— What they knew from T. V.— did-n't have a thing to do with me.—

I went back and re- upped.—

— Sure, Sai-gon is cor-rupt;— It felt bet-ter to be— here, dri -ving for the

Em - bas - sy. 'Cos here, if you can pull a string, a guy like me lives like a king; just as long as you don't be-lieve a-ny-thing.

Why God? Why this face?

Why such beau-ty___ in this place?___ I liked my mem-'ries as they were,___ but

now I'll leave___ re-mem-b'ring her, just her.___

23456789

5/09(169765)

CD Backing Tracks

1. The American Dream

(Schönberg/Boublil/Maltby)

Alain Boublil Overseas Limited.

2. Bring Him Home

(Schönberg/Boublil/Kretzmer)

Alain Boublil Music Limited/Alain Boublil Overseas Limited.

3. Bui-Doi

(Schönberg/Boublil/Maltby)

Alain Boublil Overseas Limited.

4. Empty Chairs At Empty Tables

(Schönberg/Boublil/Kretzmer)

Alain Boublil Overseas Limited.

5. Do You Hear The People Sing?

(Schönberg/Boublil/Natel/Kretzmer)

SACEM/Alain Boublil Overseas Limited.

6. Here Comes The Morning

(Schönberg/Boublil/Clark/Hardy)

Alain Boublil Overseas Limited.

7. I Will Make You Proud

(Schönberg/Boublil/Kretzmer/Hardy)

Alain Boublil Overseas Limited.

8. Martin Guerre

(Schönberg/Boublil/Clark/Hardy)

Alain Boublil Overseas Limited.

9. Master Of The House

(Schönberg/Boublil/Natel/Kretzmer)

SACEM/Alain Boublil Overseas Limited.

10. Stars

(Schönberg/Boublil/Kretzmer)

Alain Boublil Overseas Limited.

11. Who Am I?

(Schönberg/Boublil/Natel/Kretzmer)

SACEM/Alain Boublil Overseas Limited.

12. Why God Why?

(Schönberg/Boublil/Maltby)

Alain Boublil Overseas Limited.

To remove your CD from the plastic sleeve,
lift the small lip to break the perforations.
Replace the disc after use for convenient storage.